UNDERSTANDING BI-SEXUALISM IN NIGERIA COMMUNITY LONDON

Living In Challenging Times

Table of Contents

Dedication 4

Introduction..5

    What are human rights?..5

    Universal and inalienable 5

Bisexuality 11

Lesbian, gay, bisexual, and transgender in Nigeria 14

Nigeria Law on LGBT 15

    Federal Penal Code in all northern states 17

    Shari'a law enacted by certain northern states 18

    Secular criminal law enacted by certain
    northern states 27

LGBT In Nigeria News..28

Nigeria Human Right Law..34

UNDERSTANDING BI-SEXUALISM IN NIGERIA COMMUNITY LONDON

© 2012

Dedication

I dedicate this book to everyone still hiding their true
identity

Introduction

What are human rights?

Human rights are rights inherent to all human beings, whatever our nationality, place of residence, sex, national or ethnic origin, colour, religion, language, or any other status. We are all equally entitled to our human rights without discrimination. These rights are all interrelated, interdependent and indivisible.

Universal human rights are often expressed and guaranteed by law, in the forms of treaties, customary international law, general principles and other sources of international law. International human rights law lays down obligations of Governments to act in certain ways or to refrain from certain acts, in order to promote and protect human rights and fundamental freedoms of individuals or groups.

Universal and inalienable

The principle of universality of human rights is the cornerstone of international human rights law. This principle, as first emphasized in the Universal Declaration on Human Rights in 1948, has been reiterated in numerous international human rights conventions, declarations, and resolutions. The 1993 Vienna World Conference on Human Rights, for example, noted that it is the duty of States to promote and protect all human rights and fundamental freedoms, regardless of their political, economic and cultural systems.

The modern sense of human rights can be traced to Renaissance Europe and the Protestant Reformation, alongside the disappearance of the feudal authoritarianism and religious conservativism that dominated the Middle Ages.

Human rights were defined as a result of European scholars attempting to form a "secularized version of Judeo-Christian ethics". Although ideas of rights and liberty have existed in some form for much of human history, they do not resemble the modern conception of human rights. According to Jack Donnelly, in the ancient world, "traditional societies typically have had elaborate systems of duties... conceptions of justice, political legitimacy, and human flourishing that sought to realize human dignity, flourishing, or well-being entirely independent of human rights. These institutions and practices are alternative to, rather than different formulations of, human rights". The most commonly held view is that concept of human rights evolved in the West, and that while earlier cultures had important ethical concepts, they generally lacked a concept of human rights. For example, McIntyre argues there is no word for "right" in any language before 1400. Medieval charters of liberty such as the English Magna Carta were not charters of human rights, rather they were the foundation and constituted a form of limited political and legal agreement to address specific political circumstances, in the case of Magna Carta later being recognised in the course of early modern debates about rights. One of the oldest records of human rights is the statute of Kalisz (1264), giving privileges to the Jewish minority in the Kingdom of Poland such as protection from discrimination and hate speech. The basis of most modern legal interpretations of human rights can be traced back to recent European history.

The Twelve Articles (1525) are considered to be the first record of human rights in Europe. They were part of the peasants' demands raised towards the Swabian League in the German Peasants' War in Germany.

The earliest conceptualization of human rights is credited to ideas about natural rights emanating from natural law. In particular, the issue of universal rights was introduced by the examination of the rights of indigenous peoples by Spanish clerics, such as Francisco de Vitoria and Bartolomé de Las Casas. In the Valladolid debate, Juan Ginés de Sepúlveda, who maintained an Aristotelian view of humanity as divided into classes of different worth, argued with Las Casas, who argued in favor of equal rights to freedom of slavery for all humans regardless of race or religion.

Nigeria's human rights record remains poor and government officials at all levels continue to commit serious abuses.

According to the U.S. Department of State,

The most serious human rights problems during ... [2011] were the abuses committed by the militant sect known as Boko Haram, which was responsible for killings, bombings, and other attacks throughout the country, resulting in numerous deaths, injuries, and the widespread destruction of property; abuses committed by the security services with impunity, including killings, beatings, arbitrary detention, and destruction of property; and societal violence, including ethnic, regional, and religious violence. Other serious human rights problems included sporadic abridgement of citizens' right to change their government, due to some election fraud and other irregularities; politically motivated and extrajudicial killings by security forces, including summary executions; security force torture, rape, and other cruel, inhuman, or degrading treatment of prisoners, detainees, and criminal suspects; harsh and life-threatening prison and detention center conditions; arbitrary arrest and detention; prolonged pretrial detention; denial of fair public trial; executive influence on the judiciary and judicial corruption; infringements on citizens' privacy rights; restrictions on freedom of speech, press, assembly, religion, and movement; official corruption; violence and discrimination against women; child abuse; female genital mutilation ...; the killing of children suspected of witchcraft; child sexual exploitation; ethnic, regional, and religious discrimination; trafficking in persons for the purpose of prostitution and forced labor; discrimination against persons with disabilities; discrimination based on sexual orientation and gender identity; vigilante killings; forced and bonded labor; and child labor.

Twelve northern states have adopted some form of Shari'a into their criminal statutes: Bauchi, Borno,Gombe, Jigawa, Kaduna, Kano, Katsina, Kebbi, Niger, Sokoto, Yobe, and Zamfara. The Shari'a criminal laws apply to those who voluntarily consent to the jurisdiction of the Shari'a courts and to all Muslims. It provides harsh sentences for, among other crimes, alcohol consumption, infidelity, same-sex sexual activity, and theft, including amputation, lashing, stoning, and long prison terms.

Some Christian pastors in Nigeria were reported in 2009 of being involved in the torturing and killing of children accused of witchcraft. In the decade ending in 2009, over 1,000 children were murdered as "witches". Those pastors, in an effort to distinguish themselves from the competition, were accused of decrying witchcraft in an effort to establish their "credientials".

Bisexuality

Bisexuality is romantic attraction, sexual attraction or behavior toward males and females. The term is mainly used in the context of human attraction to denote romantic or sexual feelings toward men and women. Pansexuality may or may not be subsumed under bisexuality, as the terms are often treated as synonyms and people may consider bisexuality, like pansexuality, to encompass romantic or sexual attraction to all gender identities or romantic or sexual attraction to a person irrespective of that person's biological sex or gender.

Bisexuality is one of the three main classifications of sexual orientation, along with a heterosexual and a homosexual orientation, all a part of the heterosexual–homosexual continuum. People who have a distinct but not exclusive sexual preference for one sex over the other may identify themselves as bisexual.

Bisexuality has been observed in various human societies and elsewhere in the animal kingdom throughout recorded history. The term *bisexuality*, however, like the terms *hetero-* and *homosexuality*, was coined in the 19th century.

UK

In the BBC TV science fiction show *Torchwood*, several of the main characters appear to have fluid sexuality. Most prominent among these is Captain Jack Harkness, a pansexual who is the lead character and an otherwise conventional science fiction action hero. Within the logic of the show, where characters can also interact with alien species, producers sometimes use the term "omnisexual" to describe him. Jack's ex, Captain John Hart is also bisexual. Of his female exes, significantly at least one ex-wife and at least one woman with whom he has had a child have been indicated. Some critics draw the conclusion that the series more often shows Jack with men than women. Creator Russell T Davies says one of pitfalls of writing a bisexual character is you "fall into the trap" of "only having them sleep with men" He describes of the show's fourth series, "You'll see the full range of his appetites, in a really properly done way." The preoccupation with bisexuality has been seen by critics as complementary to other aspects of the show's themes. For heterosexual character Gwen Cooper, for whom Jack harbors romantic feelings, the new experiences she confronts at Torchwood, in the form of "affairs and homosexuality and the threat of death", connote not only the Other but a "missing side" to the Self. Under the influence of an alien pheromone, Gwen kisses a woman in Episode 2 of the series. In Episode 1, heterosexual Owen Harper kisses a man to escape a fight when he is about to take the man's girlfriend. Quiet Toshiko Sato is in love with Owen, but has also has brief romantic relationships with a female alien and a male human. British newspaper *The Sun* ran the headline "Dr Ooh gets four gay pals" prior to the first series, describing all of *Torchwood*'s cast as being bisexual.

In the soap opera *Hollyoaks*, the otherwise heterosexual character Craig Dean has a one-off affair with John Paul McQueen

Lesbian, gay, bisexual, and transgender in Nigeria

LGBT persons in **Nigeria** face unique legal and social challenges not experienced by non-LGBT residents. The country's record on human rights, including LGBT rights, is very poor. There is no legal protection against discrimination in Nigeria — a largely conservative country of more than 170 million people, split between a mainly Muslim north and a largely Christian south. Very few LGBT persons are open about their orientation, and violence against LGBT people is frequent.

Both male and female same-sex sexual activity is illegal in Nigeria. The maximum punishment in the twelve northern states that have adopted Shari'a law is death by stoning. That law applies to all Muslims and to those who have voluntarily consented to application of the Shari'a courts. In southern Nigeria and under the secular criminal laws of northern Nigeria, the maximum punishment for same-sex sexual activity is 14 years' imprisonment. Legislation is pending to criminalize same-sex marriage throughout the country.

According to the 2007 Pew Global Attitudes Project, 97 percent of Nigerian residents believe that homosexuality is a way of life that society should not accept, which was the second-highest rate of non-acceptance in the 45 countries surveyed.

Nigeria has been widely criticized by human and civil rights organizations, as well as the United Nations, for failing to uphold, and even violating, the rights of LGBT people

Nigeria Law on LGBT

Sex acts between men are illegal under the Criminal Code that applies to southern Nigeria and carry a maximum penalty of 14 years' imprisonment. Sex acts between women are not mentioned specifically in the code, although it is arguable that the gender-neutral term "person" in Section 214 of the code includes women. Chapter 21 of that code provides in pertinent part as follows:

- Section 214.

Any person who -

(a) has carnal knowledge of any person against the order of nature; or

* * *

(c) permits a male person to have carnal knowledge of him or her against the order of nature;

is guilty of a felony, and is liable to imprisonment for fourteen years.

- Section 215.

Any person who attempts to commit any of the offences defined in the last preceding section is guilty of a felony and is liable to imprisonment for seven years. The offender cannot be arrested without a warrant.

- Section 217.

Any male person who, whether in public or private, commits any act of gross indecency with another male person, or procures another male person to commit any act of gross indecency with him, or attempts to procure the commission of any such act by any male person with himself or with another male person, whether in public or private, is guilty of a felony and is liable to imprisonment for three years. The offender cannot be arrested without a warrant.

Federal Penal Code in all northern states

Section 284 of the Penal Code (Northern States) Federal Provisions Act, which applies to all states in northern Nigeria, provides that:

Whoever has carnal intercourse against the order of nature with any man [or] woman ... shall be punished with imprisonment for a term which may extend to fourteen years and shall also be liable to fine.

Section 405 provides that a male person who dresses or is attired in the fashion of a woman in a public place or who practises sodomy as a means of livelihood or as a profession is a "vagabond". Under Section 407, the punishment is a maximum of one year's imprisonment or a fine, or both.

Section 405 also provides that an "incorrigible vagabond" is "any person who after being convicted as a vagabond commits any of the offences which will render him liable to be convicted as such again". The punishment under Section 408 is a maximum of two years' imprisonment or a fine, or both.

Shari'a law enacted by certain northern states

Twelve northern states have adopted some form of Shari'a into their criminal statutes: Bauchi, Borno, Gombe, Jigawa, Kaduna, Kano, Katsina, Kebbi, Niger, Sokoto, Yobe, and Zamfara. The Shari'a criminal laws apply to those who voluntarily consent to the jurisdiction of the Shari'a courts and to all Muslims.

Meaning of sodomy

In the states of Kaduna and Yobe, "sodomy" is committed by "[w]hoever has anal coitus with any man".

In the states of Kano and Katsina, "sodomy" is committed by "[w]hoever has carnal intercourse against the order of nature with any man or woman through her rectum".

In the states of Bauchi, Gombe, Jigawa, Sokoto, and Zamfara, "sodomy" is committed by "[w]hoever has carnal intercourse against the order of nature with any man or woman".

Punishment for offense of sodomy

In the states of Gombe, Jigawa, and Zamfara, a person who commits the offence of sodomy shall be punished:

(a) with caning of one hundred lashes if unmarried, and shall also be liable to imprisonment for the term of one year; or

(b) if married with stoning to death (rajm).

In the state of Kano, a person who commits the offence of sodomy shall be punished:

(a) with caning of one hundred lashes if unmarried, and shall also be liable to imprisonment for the term of one year; or

(b) if married or has been previously married with stoning to death (rajm).

In the state of Bauchi, a person who commits the offence of sodomy "shall be punished with stoning to death (rajm) or by any other means decided by the state".

In the states of Kaduna, Katsina, Kebbi, and Yobe, a person who commits the offence of sodomy "shall be punished with stoning to death (rajm)".

In the state of Sokoto, a person who commits the offence of sodomy shall be punished:

(a) with stoning to death;

(b) if the act is committed by a minor on an adult person the adult person shall be punished by way of ta'azir which may extend to 100 lashes and minor with correctional punishment.

In Sokoto, "ta'azir" means "a discretionary punishment for offence whose punishment is not specified".

Meaning of lesbianism

In the states of Bauchi, Gombe, Jigawa, Kaduna, Kano, Katsina, Kebbi, Sokoto, Yobe, and Zamfara, lesbianism is committed by "[w]hoever, being a woman, engages another woman in carnal intercourse through her sexual organ or by means of stimulation or sexual excitement of one another." Bauchi, Jigawa, Katsina, Kebbi, Sokoto, Yobe and Zamfara states include the following official explanation: "The offence is committed by the unnatural fusion of the female sexual organs and/or by the use of natural or artificial means to stimulate or attain sexual satisfaction or excitement."

Punishment for offence of lesbianism

In the states of Gombe, Jigawa, Kebbi, Sokoto, Yobe, and Zamfara, a person who commits the offence of lesbianism "shall be punished with caning which may extend to fifty lashes and in addition be sentenced to a term of imprisonment which may extend to six months".

In the state of Bauchi, a person who commits the offence of lesbianism "shall be punished with caning which may extend to fifty lashes and in addition be sentenced to a term of imprisonment which may extend to up to five years".

In the state of Kaduna, the punishment for committing the offence of lesbianism is ta'azir, which means "any punishment not provided for by way of hadd or qisas"."Hadd" means "punishment that is fixed by Islamic law"."Qisas" includes "punishments inflicted upon offenders by way of retaliation for causing death/injuries to a person"

In the states of Kano and Katsina, the punishment for committing the offence of lesbianism is stoning to death.

Meaning of gross indecency

In the state of Kaduna, a person commits an act of gross indecency "in public, exposure of nakedness in public and other related acts of similar nature capable of corrupting public morals".

In the states of Kano and Katsina, a person commits an act of gross indency "by way of kissing in public, exposure of nakedness in public and other related acts of similar nature in order to corrupt public morals".

In the state of Gombe, a person commits an act of gross indecency by committing "any sexual offence against the normal or usual standards of behaviour".

The states of Bauchi, Jigawa, Kebbi, Sokoto, Yobe, and Zamfara do not define gross indecency. Their laws instead say: "Whoever commits an act of gross indecency upon the person of another without his consent or by the use of force or threat compels a person to join with him in the commission of such act shall be punished".

Punishment for offence of gross indecency

A person who commits the offence of gross indecency "shall be punished with caning which may extend to forty lashes and may be liable to imprisonment for a term not exceeding one year and may also be liable to fine".

In the state of Bauchi, a person who commits the offence of gross indecency "shall be punished with caning which may extend to forty lashes and may be liable to imprisonment for a term not exceeding seven years and may also be liable to fine".

In the state of Kaduna, the punishment for committing the offence of gross indecency is ta'azir, which means "any punishment not provided for by way of hadd or qisas"."Hadd" means "punishment that is fixed by Islamic law"."Qisas" includes "punishments inflicted upon offenders by way of retaliation for causing death/injuries to a person".

In the state of Sokoto, a person who commits the offence of gross indecency "shall be punished with caning which may extend to forty lashes or may be liable to imprisonment for a term not exceeding one year, or both, and may also be liable to fine".

Meanings of vagabond and incorrigible vagabond

In the states of Bauchi, Gombe, Jigawa, Kaduna, Kano, Katsina, Kebbi, Sokoto, Yobe, and Zamfara, "any male person who dresses or is attired in the fashion of a woman in a public place or who practises sodomy as a means of livelihood or as a profession" is a vagabond.

In the states of Kano and Katsina, "any female person who dresses or is attired in the fashion of a man in a public place" is a vagabond.

In the states of Bauchi, Gombe, Jigawa, Kaduna, Kano, Katsina, Kebbi, Sokoto, Yobe, and Zamfara, an "incorrigible vagabond" is "any person who after being convicted as a vagabond commits any of the offences which will render him liable to be convicted as such again".

Punishment for being a vagabond or incorrigible vagabond

In the states of Bauchi, Gombe, Jigawa, Katsina, Kebbi, Sokoto, Yobe, and Zamfara, "[w}hoever is convicted as being a vagabond shall be punished with imprisonment for a term which may extend to one year and shall be liable to caning which may extend to thirty lashes".[127]

In the state of Kano, "[w}hoever is convicted as being a vagabond shall be punished with imprisonment for a term which may extend to eight months and shall be liable to caning which may extend to thirty-five lashes".

In the state of Kaduna, the punishment for being convicted as a vagabond is ta'azir, which means "any punishment not provided for by way of hadd or qisas"."Hadd" means "punishment that is fixed by

Islamic law"."Qisas" includes "punishments inflicted upon offenders by way of retaliation for causing death/injuries to a person".

In the states of Gombe, Jigawa, Katsina, Kebbi, Sokoto, Yobe, and Zamfara, "[w]hoever is convicted as being an incorrigible vagabond shall be punished with imprisonment for a term which may extend to two years and shall be liable to caning which may extend to fifty lashes".

In the state of Bauchi, "[w]hoever is convicted as being an incorrigible vagabond shall be punished with imprisonment for a term which may extend to two years and shall be liable to caning which may extend to forty lashes".

In the state of Kano, "[w]hoever is convicted as being an incorrigible vagabond shall be punished with imprisonment for a term which may extend to one year and shall be liable to caning which may extend to fifty lashes".

In the state of Kaduna, the punishment for being convicted as an incorrigible vagabond is ta'azir

Secular criminal law enacted by certain northern states

Same-sex sexual activities

In the state of Bormo, a person who "engages in ... lesbianism, homosexual act ... in the State commits an offence". A person who "engages in sexual intercourse with another person of the same gender shall upon conviction be punished with death".

Males immitating the behavioural attitudes of women

In the state of Kano, a person who "being a male gender who acts, behaves or dresses in a manner which imitate the behavioural attitude of women shall be guilty of an offence and upon conviction, be sentenced to 1 year imprisonment or a fine of N10,000 or both".[

Nigeria: Advisory on Proposed Ban on Gay Marriage in Nigeria, Africa's Most Populous Country
01/30/2006

IGLHRC is deeply concerned and actively investigating reports coming out of Nigeria regarding a new bill that has been introduced for consideration by the National Assembly. The bill will criminalize same-sex marriage and impose a penalty of five years imprisonment for anyone involved in such a union. The introduction of such a bill is deeply disturbing, given its redundancy (only opposite sex marriages are currently performed in the country) and the lack of any movement among Nigerian gays and lesbians for marriage rights. Clearly the proposed law is an attempt to further marginalize an increasingly vocal minority.

Human rights activists are even more appalled by rumors that the bill will also criminalize gay "advocacy" and "relationships". While it is still unclear what such prohibitions actually mean, a worst-case scenario could include the criminalization of any discussion on gay liberation, newspaper articles debating sexual rights and any meetings—political or social—of gay and lesbian people. Clearly this would constitute a major violation of international and regional human rights standards and challenge provisions to freedom of speech, assembly and association in Nigeria's own constitution.

The bill, initiated by the office of President Olesugun Obasanjo, who is running for re-election, comes on the heels of a number of events in Africa that are clearly threatening to the homophobic status quo. The protection of the right of same-sex couples to marry by the South Africa Constitutional Court sent a message of equality throughout the continent. The Office of the President has also cited reports that gay rights activists "stormed" the International Conference on AIDS and Sexually Transmitted Diseases in Africa (ICASA) in Abuja in December of last year demanding their rights. A group of LGBT and sexual rights activists from across the African continent did in fact participate in the ICASA conference, respectfully asking governments, donors and civil society to pay greater attention to the HIV/AIDS vulnerability of men who have sex with men and women who have sex with women on the African continent.

IGLHRC is working closely with LGBT and sexual rights advocates in Nigeria and the rest of Africa to develop an effective, African-led strategy that questions the knee-jerk conservatism and religious extremism that is fueling this move. IGLHRC is joining forces with the substantial human rights, women's rights, and progressive religious communities in Nigeria.

For more information, contact Cary Alan Johnson, Senior Specialist for Africa at the International Gay and Lesbian Human Rights Commission, cjohnson@iglhrc.org, 212.216.1849.

http://www.iglhrc.org/cgi-bin/iowa/article/takeaction/resourcecenter/246.html

Nigeria: Dispatch from Bauchi on the Case of 18 Men Arrested for Gender Transgression
11/13/2007

A case involving eighteen men arrested and charged with cross-dressing in Bauchi State, Nigeria was adjourned on October 8, 2007 after defense lawyers complained of not having received key legal documents.

The 18 men were arrested on August 5th, 2007, while attending a party at the Benko Hotel, in the Yelwa area of Bauchi—a state in Northern Nigeria that has adopted Islamic law. The men have been charged under Article 372 Sec 2(E) of the Bauchi State Islamic Penal Code with "vagrancy," which includes prohibitions against cross-dressing and the practice of sodomy. The first hearing in the case was held at the Tunde Alkali Area court in Bauchi. Thereafter the case was moved to the Upper Shari'a court in the same city.

Despite the charges, the men were not dressed in women's clothes at the time of their arrests, and the police have reported that only a few items of women's clothing were found in their belongings. IGLHRC is concerned that the men are being targeted because of increased homophobia in Nigeria, as evidenced by attempts during the last parliamentary session to pass a draconian bill to criminalize gatherings of LGBT people.

Though all 18 men have been released on bail, they have been refused permission to leave Bauchi State. This is causing the men great hardship, since only five of them are residents of the state and the majority are students. "I have not been able to attend classes and/or write exams, which I need to do in order to be admitted to graduate school," complained Tahir T. one of the detainees.

Joel Nana, IGLHRC Program Associate for West and Southern Africa who has been monitoring the case, stressed that requiring the men to remain in Bauchi, "puts them at risk of potential harassment and violence by the local population which has already manifested its disdain for the men." Crowds threw stones at the men and their lawyers at the first hearing, requiring police to fire bullets into the air to disperse the crowd.

"The courts are behaving as if the men have already been judged as guilty," said Joseph Akoro, Director of The Independent Project (TIP), a Nigerian LGBT organization that has been present at each of the hearings in the case.

The next hearing in the case is scheduled for November 29, 2007. IGLHRC is working with a coalition of organizations and funders, including Global Rights, the Astraea Foundation, and the International Commission of Jurists-Kenya, to ensure that local human rights and LGBT organizations are able to effectively provide legal and political support to the detainees. IGLHRC has also filed a formal complaint with the UN Working Group on Arbitrary Detention.

http://www.iglhrc.org/cgi-bin/iowa/article/takeaction/resourcecenter/342.html

Nigeria Human Right Law

Chapter II
Fundamental Objectives and Directive Principles of State Policy

13. It shall be the duty and responsibility of all organs of government, and of all authorities and persons, exercising legislative, executive or judicial powers, to conform to, observe and apply the provisions of this Chapter of this Constitution.

14. (1) The Federal Republic of Nigeria shall be a State based on the principles of democracy and social justice.

(2) It is hereby, accordingly, declared that:

(a) sovereignty belongs to the people of Nigeria from whom government through this Constitution derives all its powers and authority;

(b) the security and welfare of the people shall be the primary purpose of government: and

(c) the participation by the people in their government shall be ensured in accordance with the provisions of this Constitution.

(3) The composition of the Government of the Federation or any of its agencies and the conduct of its affairs shall be carried out in such a manner as to reflect the federal character of Nigeria and the need to promote national unity, and also to command national loyalty, thereby ensuring that there shall be no predominance of persons from a few State or from a few ethnic or other sectional groups in that Government or in any of its agencies.

(4) The composition of the Government of a State, a local government council, or any of the agencies of such Government or council, and the conduct of the affairs of the Government or council or such agencies shall be carried out in such manner as to recognise the diversity of the people within its area of authority and the need to promote a sense of belonging and loyalty among all the people of the Federation.

15. (1) The motto of the Federal Republic of Nigeria shall be Unity and Faith, Peace and Progress.

(2) Accordingly, national integration shall be actively encouraged, whilst discrimination on the grounds of place of origin, sex, religion, status, ethnic or linguistic association or ties shall be prohibited.

(3) For the purpose of promoting national integration, it shall be the duty of the State to:

(a) provide adequate facilities for and encourage free mobility of people, goods and services throughtout the Federation.

(b) secure full residence rights for every citizen in all parts of the Federation.

(c) encourage inter-marriage among persons from different places of origin, or of different religious, ethnic or linguistic association or ties; and

(d) promote or encourage the formation of associations that cut across ethnic, linguistic, religious and or other sectional barriers.

(4) The State shall foster a feeling of belonging and of involvement among the various people of the Federation, to the end that loyalty to the nation shall override sectional loyalties.

(5) The State shall abolish all corrupt practices and abuse of power.

16. (1) The State shall, within the context of the ideals and objectives for which provisions are made in this Constitution.

(a) harness the resources of the nation and promote national prosperity and an efficient, a dynamic and self-reliant economy;

(b) control the national economy in such manner as to secure the maximum welfare, freedom and happiness of every citizen on the basis of social justice and equality of status and opportunity;

(c) without prejudice to its right to operate or participate in areas of the economy, other than the major sectors of the economy, manage and operate the major sectors of the economy;

(d) without prejudice to the right of any person to participate in areas of the economy within the major sector of the economy, protect the right of every citizen to engage in any economic activities outside the major sectors of the economy.

(2) The State shall direct its policy towards ensuring:

(a) the promotion of a planned and balanced economic development;

(b) that the material resources of the nation are harnessed and distributed as best as possible to serve the common good;

(c) that the economic system is not operated in such a manner as to permit the concentration of wealth or the means of production and exchange in the hands of few individuals or of a group; and

(d) that suitable and adequate shelter, suitable and adequate food, reasonable national minimum living wage, old age care and pensions, and unemployment, sick benefits and welfare of the disabled are provided for all citizens.

(3) A body shall be set up by an Act of the National Assembly which shall have power;

(a) to review, from time to time, the ownership and control of business enterprises operating in Nigeria and make recommendations to the President on same; and

(b) to administer any law for the regulation of the ownership and control of such enterprises.

(4) For the purposes of subsection (1) of this section -

(a) the reference to the "major sectors of the economy" shall be construed as a reference to such economic activities as may, from time to time, be declared by a resolution of each House of the National Assembly to be managed and operated exclusively by the Government of the Federation, and until a resolution to the contrary is made by the National Assembly, economic activities being operated exclusively by the Government of the Federation on the date immediately preceding the day when this section comes into force, whether directly or through the agencies of a statutory or other corporation or company, shall be deemed to be major sectors of the economy;

(b) "economic activities" includes activities directly concerned with the production, distribution and exchange of weather or of goods and services; and

(c) "participate" includes the rendering of services and supplying of goods.

17. (1) The State social order is founded on ideals of Freedom, Equality and Justice.

(2) In furtherance of the social order-

(a) every citizen shall have equality of rights, obligations and opportunities before the law;

(b) the sanctity of the human person shall be recognised and human dignity shall be maintained and enhanced;

(c) governmental actions shall be humane;

(d) exploitation of human or natural resources in any form whatsoever for reasons, other than the good of the community, shall be prevented; and

(e) the independence, impartiality and integrity of courts of law, and easy accessibility thereto shall be secured and maintained.

(3) The State shall direct its policy towards ensuring that-

(a) all citizens, without discrimination on any group whatsoever, have the opportunity for securing adequate means of livelihood as well as adequate opportunity to secure suitable employment;

(b) conditions of work are just and humane, and that there are adequate facilities for leisure and for social, religious and cultural life;

(c) the health, safety and welfare of all persons in employment are safeguarded and not endangered or abused;

(d) there are adequate medical and health facilities for all persons:

(e) there is equal pay for equal work without discrimination on account of sex, or on any other ground whatsoever;

(f) children, young persons and the age are protected against any exploitation whatsoever, and against moral and material neglect;

(g) provision is made for public assistance in deserving cases or other conditions of need; and

(h) the evolution and promotion of family life is encouraged.

18. (1) Government shall direct its policy towards ensuring that there are equal and adequate educational opportunities at all levels.

(2) Government shall promote science and technology

(3) Government shall strive to eradicate illiteracy; and to this end Government shall as and when practicable provide

(a) free, compulsory and universal primary education;

(b) free secondary education;

(c) free university education; and

(d) free adult literacy programme.

19. The foreign policy objectives shall be -

(a) promotion and protection of the national interest;

(b) promotion of African integration and support for African unity;

(c) promotion of international co-operation for the consolidation of universal peace and mutual respect among all nations and elimination of discrimination in all its manifestations;

(d) respect for international law and treaty obligations as well as the seeking of settlement of international disputes by negotiation, mediation, conciliation, arbitration and adjudication; and

(e) promotion of a just world economic order.

20. The State shall protect and improve the environment and safeguard the water, air and land, forest and wild life of Nigeria.

21. The State shall -

(a) protect, preserve and promote the Nigerian cultures which enhance human dignity and are consistent with the fundamental objectives as provided in this Chapter; and

(b) encourage development of technological and scientific studies which enhance cultural values.

22. The press, radio, television and other agencies of the mass media shall at all times be free to uphold the fundamental objectives contained in this Chapter and uphold the responsibility and accountability of the Government to the people.

23. The national ethics shall be Discipline, Integrity, Dignity of Labour, Social, Justice, Religious Tolerance, Self-reliance and Patriotism.

24. It shall be the duty of every citizen to -

(a) abide by this Constitution, respect its ideals and its institutions, the National Flag, the National Anthem, the National Pledge, and legitimate authorities;

(b) help to enhance the power, prestige and good name of Nigeria, defend Nigeria and render such national service as may be required;

(c) respect the dignity of other citizens and the rights and legitimate interests of others and live in unity and harmony and in the spirit of common brotherhood;

(d) make positive and useful contribution to the advancement, progress and well-being of the community where he resides;

(e) render assistance to appropriate and lawful agencies in the maintenance of law and order; and

(f) declare his income honestly to appropriate and lawful agencies and pay his tax promptly.